Content

Millionaire

How to create content that changes people's

lives and generate a fortune

Table Of Contents

Introduction

More and more content is produced by agencies, journalists, PR people, small- and medium enterprises that will never be consumed by their target audience. The reason for this is that people have good intention to create content but they lack strategy in the research, creation, optimization and monetization part. I have been there too! I also created content that didn't reach the right audience, because I just created for creation's sake. I deeply believe that content is king, therefore I created and still create content for different channels. Based on data through Google analytics, I realized that the people who I want to help were not finding my content, and this was my personal turning point. I recognized that strategic content is the answer, instead of just focusing on creating more articles. In order to shorten the learning curve and help other people, I decided to write this book and help other content creators, authors, PR staff, marketing people and small- and medium enterprise owners with their content marketing strategy. So that they can help their own audience with excellent content and on the way, also create a fortune.

The reality is that the world of content marketing is changing rapidly. Voice search, performance or influencer marketing and other buzz words are coming every day into this market and are changing the rules of the past. Blockchain is also becoming more and more important and it also changes the rules of marketing. Technology now enables automatization of content creation and also helps with the monetization of content.

These days there is this big opportunity to participate at content marketing and help other people with the right strategy. You have to know what your audience wants before you start generating your content. Just because you think your audience is interested in this topic is not a big enough reason for you to start writing about it. In order to survive, you need a strategic plan on how to research about your target audience. This is not enough: You also have to know which channels your audience use and also how to leverage your content to reach a bigger audience. The new model of content marketing is all about creation, monetization and also distribution of your own content. You have to make sure that you put your message on the right channels. This means that you not only have to be good at the content creation, but also have to understand business models and how distribution works.

I had a very humble beginning when it comes to content. For a long time, my main intention was on the creation part: I worked for newspapers, magazines, a TV station and online platforms before I started as the digital editor at a company, which focuses mainly on content marketing. Here I realized that I had no clue what I was doing and then learned excessively about this topic through different departments (magazines, video, social media, distribution, project management, advertisement). This experience thought me how to structure content so that it is found online, how to earn money with it and also how to reach bigger audiences, all of which I'm going to cover in this book.

Everything that I'm teaching here is also possible for you. I'm not that different from you, I would guess you may have much more talent when it comes to writing skills compared with me. More important than your writing skills is your intention to help other people with your content; if you already have this main focus, the book will scale your results through a strategic approach of your work.

The reason why you should keep reading this book is that it will change how to think about content and help you get a better life. In the process you will not only create content that change the life of your audience and make you a better person but also generate you a fortune. This is what I call a content millionaire – somebody who changes people's lives and generates a fortune on the process. This book will teach you how to achieve this.

Chapter one is about the general idea of content marketing. Here I give a definition and explain the meaning of content marketing and how it changed over time. **Chapter two** is my own story how I started from creating simple PDFs and sharing them on Facebook groups, to becoming what one client called me "a content machine" (which really sounds heavier than it is and I will also show you how you can simply do it yourself). **Chapter three** is all about the big picture framework and how to implement your content marketing strategy. Here I explain the six steps to follow in order to make sure that you land your content on your audience. **Chapter four** is about *Content Analysis and Research*. You have to find out based on data what your audience is looking, reading, and searching for. Based on this data, you're going to create your content plan, what topics you're going to publish and when. After identifying the main topics and keywords of your target audience, **chapter five** will be about content creation. There are many ways to create your content (whitepapers, pdfs, newsletter, blogs, videos and much more) and different options of which one to use first. **Chapter six** is about content monetization and how to earn money with your content pieces. **Chapter seven** is about content optimization and basic SEO rules, so that search-engines like Google really love what you produce. **Chapter eight** is all about traffic and the different models on how to generate it. You will learn the main ways how to generate traffic and buzz around your content and also attract the right people to your content piece. **Chapter nine** is all about content leverage and how to include the media and also work together with businesses and NGOs to reach a bigger audience with your content. **Chapter ten** is a FAQ of the most common questions that I found based on the topic of content marketing. **Chapter eleven** is about a quick start and taking your next steps. I know that that the topic of content marketing can be overwhelming. So, make sure that you start with little steps and make progress on a daily basis.

Chapter 1: Why you need this book

'Content is king' is a widely heard statement by companies but the reality often times look different. The main struggle and the biggest problems that content creators have is the so called *content gap*. This is the gap between creation of the content and being found by their main audience. Often times, content is "just" created and then the work flow stops and hope-marketing (a term by Jeff Walker; a famous marketing guru who invented Product Launch Formula that teaches basically how to sell products and services online) sets in. The content creators just hope that their audience will find their piece of content – which is by the way the worst way of approaching marketing. It is neither strategic nor pro-active, it`s just the opposite. Writing a blog post on your personal blog is a great way to share your knowledge and wisdom, but honestly how often did you revisit this blog post? Often times, content creators create blog posts and then they disappear in the archives of our blog. This is not a very efficient use of this content piece, instead think about each content that you create as an asset that you, from time to time, reuse for your own needs. Later on, we will go much deeper how to do this in detail. First of all, I want to convince you to take your content marketing approach more strategically and forget about hope marketing. If you follow hope marketing, you will always depend on other people's agenda or the next paycheck. In order to solve this problem, you have to be more strategic about how to structure and also distribute your own content on the right channels. Before going into more details about how to structure your content, I want to explain in more detail about content marketing in general.

Content marketing basically means content-driven marketing that helps readers or enables them to solve their daily problems. Content Marketing is one instrument to reach your audience, share your own knowledge, and lead to the sale of a product or service.

The idea of content marketing is already much older. In the old days, the formats of content were very clear: Newspaper and printed magazine articles were the first steps of content marketing, even if nobody called it so at that time. Through the invention of radio and television, the portfolio of content marketing grew, even sound and also moving pictures are included as content pieces. The world wide web changed the whole game and also how content marketing works as industry. These days, content is not only in written form, but also as MP3 and video formats, which are often times mixed. Multimedia versions of content are business-as-usual, and technology enables automatization and individualization of marketing funnels. The good thing is that through technology, it becomes easier to become a content creator yourself, distribute your own content and accept credit card payments. Here are some examples on how easy it is to implement your content marketing strategy:

When you search about content on how to become a Forbes Contributor you will definitely read some of the content of Josh Steimle. Maybe you've never heard of him but he is one of the leading experts when it comes to the topic about how to become a contributor at Forbes. When you research about how to become a Forbes contributor, you will definitely come across one of his blog posts where he strategically teaches the strategies on the topic. He is doing this with purpose because he organizes a Masterclass that people can book in order to get personal coaching. He not only has a big following and much valued blog posts but he also has a newsletter where he gives great value, too. Great example of how specified content pieces can lead people into your sales funnel. Important here to mention that all strategies first teach in a great way and deliver much free value. The selling part is not the first priority, but the delivering value is just more important.

Podcast work the same. Tim Ferriss, bestselling author of Tools of Titans and the 4-hour-work-week, interviews in his podcast The Tim Ferris Show entrepreneurs who either launch a product themselves or offer some kind of service that people can choose to do. These entrepreneurs speak about topics like time management, pitching investors or how to start a successful business. Very valuable for anybody who is interested in general knowledge about entrepreneurship, and also a great tool in order to implement your content marketing strategy. Most of the content is for free and Tim Ferris is delivering much content on his website.

Content marketing also works very well for authors. This is something that the author of the bestselling book *The Alchemist* Paulo Coelho is doing very well. *The Alchemist* is one of the most often translated and printed books of history. Paulo has a newsletter with a huge subscriber list and informs his readers about the creation process or topics that are important for him. He not only writes his newsletter but also writes columns in print magazines about topics like spirituality and other topics that are related to his books.

When Michelle Obama visited Germany in the year 2018 and gave rare interviews about her new book, this was also content marketing. In the interviews, she talked about many topics that she covered in her book. People who read the interview were also interested in the book and at the end of the interview, got more information about it. You don't have to be the first lady in order to do this. Everybody can do this with related topics. If you publish your own book, you should also think about how to reach out to journalists and offer them material about the content of your book.

When Marvel's Avengers releases a new trailer about their upcoming movie, then this is also content marketing. Behind the set scenes and interviews with the main characters are also a very effective way of using video pieces to create buzz around the upcoming movie. The main aim of these content pieces is to create buzz and motivate you to buy a cinema ticket.

Larry King is a legend when it comes to journalism. He is one of the most well-known journalists in the U.S. and has interviewed people like the Dalai Lama. Together with the marketing expert Brendon Burchard, he produced a video online course about Larry's long experience as a communicator. Within the Content Marketing strategy, there were a series of interviews and also a podcast where Brendon promoted this course. Video content pieces can be very powerful if you integrate it into your marketing mix.

The good news is that everybody can do this. You don't have to be a big celebrity, guru or politician in order to take these approaches. Everybody can and should do this to promote their own physical or digital products and services like books or consulting, to sell. It is not important how big your numbers are, more important is that you start creating content and sharing it in a strategic way and bringing people into your sales funnel.

The bad news is that it is harder to get the attention of your audience because there are so many competitors. If I write that it was never easier to become a content creator then this is true, but is only one part of its real meaning. It just also means that everybody can enter this market without big struggles. So, more and more people are competing with really good content pieces and you have to be aware of your own unique selling proposition. Not only this fact: you also need data gathering. You have to be aware that content marketing of the 21st century means collecting and analyzing data material with digital tools.

If you really want to survive and succeed in the field of content marketing, then you need to focus on new skills like data gathering, automatization tools and also a basic understanding of business models. Many authors, me too at the beginning, just focus on the content creation part, but this thinking is too short. The people that are going to win in the long term are those who invest their time and educate themselves within the field of marketing and basic understanding of business models. Those people who can implement or at least think like entrepreneurs will win in the long-term, because the world becomes more competitive and those who understand how a business runs and also can create good content will succeed. Those folks who analyze data and check it on a regular basis will not only survive, but also win big. The people who are going to lose are those who only invest their time in improving their writing skills without thinking about the business side. I want to say that improving writing skills is very important and necessary and I also believe that the art of good writing becomes much more important in the world, but it is necessary to combine writing skills with other business skills. Why not add more experience and take a copy-writing course? Or newsletter marketing? Or basics about digital marketing?

When I first started creating my content I had no clue about marketing, target audiences and also knew nothing about business. My main intention was to create good content and nothing more but also nothing else. I got my first lecture from a mentor who thought me to acquire business skills like marketing and add it to my portfolio of skills. My mentor thought me that I should combine my writing skills with business skills to help me scale my work and reach the next level. So I started reading business books from Brian Tracy and Tony Robbins. Nevertheless, when I started working at one of the biggest publishing houses in Germany, I realized that my numbers at Google Analytic were terribly low. This was a shock for me because I understood that I was not reaching my full potential. I decided that less content which is a good fit for your target audience is better than creating more and more content that is not read at all. This was the starting point for a major shift in my development. I started attending to courses about email marketing, bought video online courses from the best marketers like Brendon Burchard, Jeff Walker, Brian Tracy and Frank Kern. I implemented their advice and all of sudden, my articles become better at Google rankings, the newsletter opening rates increased and also the click-through rate improved dramatically. People all of a sudden started to write me about how helpful my articles are. This only happened because I started to look around and ask myself who has the results that I want to achieve and I bought their products and modeled their behavior (and still do it). I really believe that you can do this too. It was not magic for me, pure opposite, it was a wild ride and I also had many obstacles that I want to share in the next chapter.

Chapter 2: My own story

Since my first internship as journalist back in 2008 until today, I write because I want to help other people with my writing. Sometimes it was tough and especially 2012 was a major turning point for me. At that time, I was working within a marketing department of a tourism agency and also had a journalism mentor who gave me advice and some counseling. Basically I sent him my articles and he gave me feedback about it. I remember one email from him that hurt me a lot because back then I was not very good at accepting criticism. He basically wrote me that my article was inefficient and not useful at all. At that time, this was shocking for me but also a door opening for massive change in my life. After being depressed and sad for about two days and also after great support of my then girlfriend (today my wife) I decided that I had to change. I had to change and acquire more skills that would help me to write more efficient and reach more people. I started reading books about business from Brian Tracy, listening to motivation videos from Les Brown and Jim Rohn and one person that helped me especially with my writing skill was the journalist Earl Nightingale and his book The Strangest Secret. Not only this, I also started to attend to workshops and seminars about public relations, digital marketing, business, leadership and much more other skills (I was constantly looking for new topics in order to grow and network with other people). One important thing was that I also started to buy video online courses by marketing experts like Brendon Burchard, Jeff Walker and Frank Kern.

These inputs really accelerated my knowledge and helped me to reach bigger audiences. Brendon Burchard taught me in his world-class course Experts academy on how to structure and create content in different formats, Jeff Walker is really the guru when it comes to monetization of products online and he teaches through his major program called Product Launch Formula, and Frank Kern is one of highest paid copywriters on the planet. Backwards this one email that I got by my journalism mentor was really the best thing that ever happened to me, because it opened my hunger for practical knowledge and a deep desire to achieve results and become a content force.

The second major turning point for me was when I saw for the first time my data at Google Analytics and how many people read my articles. I started working as Digital Editor at Territory –

Content to Results, which belongs also to one of the biggest publishing houses in Europe - Bertelsmann. Here I had the possibility to learn from different departments like social media, video, print magazines, influencer marketing and also event planing how to create content for different formats in order to reach your audience. Not only that, this experience gave me also a fundamental knowledge about how to analyse data and emphasize what content to create first with tools like Google Analytics. The low numbers of my articles shocked me and all of a sudden, I understood that I had to learn how to SEO optimize my articles for the web. This basically means that my article is built so that search engines like Google and Youtube can find my article on the web. I attended classes and spoke with experts in these fields, interviewed them and modeled their behaviour. Through constant improvement and reading what was going on in the market, my numbers also increased and I reached more and more people. This work experience helped me to structure content so it is understandable and easy to read.

Maybe you're also interested how I got my first experience with content marketing? Interestingly, it was a coincidence and back then, I even didn't know that it was really content marketing. Back on my university time, I studied Political Science on the University Trier in Germany. This subject was very time consuming because of the big reading pensum that I had to accomplish on a weekly basis. Every week students must not only read long scientific articles but also get the main message, main arguments and how the authors structure the text, we also had to always analyze the articles intensively. Back at that time, I wanted to create goodwill and help other people with my writings. This was and is until today my main intention why I'm writing. So, I started to create abstracts, around 4-5 pages; summaries about the scientific article, and posted them on relevant Facebook groups of the university. I did this for two or three weeks, until I got a message by a student. She asked me if I could give her lectures about Political Science topics and would of course also pay me for these lectures. I accepted this offer and realized the power of content marketing and how it can generate you also an income. The important aspect here is that my main intention was really to help others with my writing and not to generate a sale, but all of a sudden it helped me also to generate an income.

This is not the best part. I still posted abstracts on a regular basis and also created detailed PDFs that helped people; they were very thankful for it and especially students from abroad wrote me that they understood the scientific articles better through my abstracts. All of a sudden I became some kind of expert that people came to and asked questions. Students started to ask me questions about their papers or presentation that they needed help with. I never met these persons before but through word of mouth, they found me and asked me for advice. That is the power of content marketing. Through constantly sharing good content, people will come to you and ask for your advice and wisdom. I not only generated income through posting these PDFs but I also positioned myself as some kind of political science expert. It really sounds strange that posting two or three PDFs in different Facebook groups made me an expert that people go to, but this is the reality. If you honestly share it and give people understandable advice they will come to you and ask for help, because they combine your content with you as a person.

You can also reverse engineer this whole process. As what kind of expert do you want to be seen as? As financial expert? Than start publishing about financial topics and help people to improve their own finances. As expert about meditation? Than create content about meditation and consult people how to use meditation techniques. Do you want to be seen as an artist expert? Then write articles about painting and also answer questions that people have about the topic. This sounds like a no-brainer but honestly how many content pieces have you created about your expertise in the last six months? If it was less than six content pieces, you not yet stepped seriously into the world of content marketing and there is much place to grow. No matter how big or small your business is, content marketing will improve your positioning and leverage how many people you can reach. Even if you're just starting out, this can be implemented also with a very short or no budget at all.

These strategies helped me and also other people. I helped sports clubs and also businesses strategically improve their content performance. I'm a blackbelt taekwondo trainer and have helped taekwondo clubs to improve their online content so that they are featured in local media. I improved their press releases and sent them to newspapers and online platforms in order to be published on a local level. Not only that, I also helped small businesses to position themselves and create constantly content so that major media is interested in them. I will show you how to do this in the chapter about leveraging your own content, so that also the media is interested in your press releases. This is no magic but rather a simple and understandable approach how to reach out to journalists. Not only for other people but also for my own products. When I first launched my video online course, "Author-preneur – How to self-publish, market and sell your own book", I also created blog posts and gave major ideas away and posted them on Facebook. All of a sudden people asked me questions about the topics and started following me. Even more experienced authors than me asked me questions and wanted my advice. So, it is not about how long you do this, it is how deep you really care about the needs and struggles of your audience and how much you help them solve their urgent needs and problems.

Chapter 3: Big picture framework

In order to succeed with your content marketing strategy, there are six steps to follow in order to make sure that you land your content with your target audience:

- **Content Analysis and Research**
- **Content Generation**
- **Content Optimization**
- **Content Monetization**
- **Traffic, Traffic, Traffic (Free and paid traffic)**
- **Content Leverage**

In this chapter I will explain briefly the six steps for your own content marketing strategy and give you the big picture about them. After that I will explain the biggest obstacles that people have and how to overcome them.

1. Content Analysis and Research

The first step in order to create effective content is your analysis and research part. You have to find out based on data what your audience is looking, reading, and searching for. The good thing is that, these days, it is easier than ever. In the past, you had to create big surveys and also interview people–however through the web, it is much easier to gather information. In order to understand your audience, read Amazon reviews of the products they consume, the books they read, and the comments they write. Tools like Google Trends and Google Keyword also help to identify main keywords and topics that your audience is looking for. In order to get a deep understanding of your target audience, you can also do a short survey with the free tool at *surveymonkey.com* where you ask people to answer relevant questions.

2. Content Creation

After identifying the main topics and keywords of your target audience, you can start creating your content plan. This is a plan that you ideally create once and follow through. The most important thing is to be consistent with your content plan and publishing; i.e., once a week one original post. After writing your content plan, there are many formats to deliver them to your audience: Whitepapers, Newsletter, Videos, PDFs, ebooks, books, and much more. Always focus on your target audience and what they are comfortable with consuming. I will show you how to create and also name your content so that your readers will love and instantly identify with it and become raving fans of your style. How to reuse your content in a very efficient way so that you leverage one content piece for different channels and let it work more than once. Tools and software that will help you to become a content-creating machine and use your time more efficiently.

3. Content Optimization

Once you have published your content, you should think about it as an asset. An asset that is growing in worth over time if you do the work that is necessary for it. This means constant SEO optimization. SEO optimization basically means to structure your content so that search engines, like Google, identify your content as a valuable piece. The good thing is that when you do your research in a good way, then your chances are good that SEO optimization becomes easy. There are basic rules when it comes to headlines, pictures, videos, and also meta title that are included in your content, which are all going to be explained in this chapter. Also, trends like Voice Search are covered in this chapter. The good news is that new topics are always coming in, but when you know the fundamentals of SEO, then you can cover every topic and reach your target audience over and over again.

4. Content Monetization

Writing and publishing is easy for most people, but where it gets tough is the monetization aspect because you need a basic understanding of business models. There are basically two business models on how to earn money with your content:

1. You offer your service as a writer or content marketer and generate content for a customer (which is time-consuming and highly competitive) or

2. You create yourself sales funnels and distribute your own content through intelligent technology (you can leverage your time, money, and reach bigger audiences).

Basically, there is this campaign model: You offer free advice, and then at some point, you charge people for deeper training. That's basically how to charge your audience. The chapter is all about how to use a Content Management System (CMS), collect E-Mail addresses and sell and purchase products.

5. Traffic, Traffic, Traffic (Free and paid traffic)

After the content is written and published, we have to create traffic in order to generate buzz. In order to generate traffic, there are generally three ways: Free traffic, paid traffic, and Joint Venture (JV) traffic. Free traffic is generated through organic search from your social media channels. When you post your content piece on your Facebook News feed, your friends see this article. The reach of your content piece is at the same time limited because you only reach your friends on social media. In order to scale and reach a bigger audience, you have to buy an advertisement on Facebook, LinkedIn, Google, or even start an Influencer marketing campaign. The third option is to create traffic through Joint Venture partnerships. First, identify a Content

Creator who serves the same target audience as you. Partner up with him, introduce yourself as a content creator for the same topic, and offer your own products.

6. Content Leverage

As Content Creators, we are so obsessed with creating new content that we don't look at our already published content. In my opinion, already published contents are assets that we have to check from time to time and reschedule in our daily agenda. If you don't have a strategy, this will help you reorganize and rethink your already published content. Offer your expertise and your content to journalists, businesses, NGOs, and also podcasters in order to scale your reach. See yourself as resources for your topic and offer people your advice. Pitching to journalists and becoming a contributor are effective ways to reach a bigger audience and leverage your content. You not only position yourself within the media, but you also generate traffic to your contributor page from the media.

7. Main questions

This chapter is all about the small and also big questions that people have related to content marketing. I collected questions in forums, asked people and also made a survey about their main struggles and obstacles when it comes to content creation. In this chapter, I'm answering most of them and if you just read one chapter than maybe that one would be a good one.

8. First steps

After explaining so much I understand when readers say "I'm overwhelmed and don't know where to start". That's the reason why I wrote this chapter about your first steps that you can do in order to start your career as a content creator. It can be also a summary of the entire steps within this book, of course not that detailed but useful for an overview.

These are the eight chapters within the book. Important for implementation are the chapters one to six where you get a fundamental understanding about the work-flow. For many people the work-flow for content generation sounds very good but they never implement it in their daily action plan because of four main reasons:

Obstacle #1: You don't have the resources (either time or money) to follow this work flow

This is one of the major obstacles that small- and medium size enterprises and also solo-entrepreneurs have. They don't have the time or money to create content within their company and therefore also can't outsource it to somebody else. Honestly, this is just an excuse not to focus on content marketing, because if you really deeply care about your topic you have to see it as necessity to share it with other people. If you're really convinced about your product or service (which I hope you are) then it is your duty to share it through content. Always think in terms of what people miss when they don't know about your product or service. What opportunities and possibilities are they going to miss? There are easy ways on how to implement a basic content strategy for your own company. I will show you a one year content plan that everybody can follow through without spending one penny.

One year content plan:

For each month you create one unique blog post that you can reuse for different channels. One unique blog post every month is realistic for even the most busy people, it can be a short article around 300-400 words. In the chapter of content generation, I will go more in depth about how to organize and structure your articles. Even if you don't have authors within your team, you can implement and at least create your content plan.

For each month, create pictures that are free at https://pablo.buffer.com and use them for your blog post, Instagram, Pinterest and Twitter Account.

Obstacle #2: You can`t see a direct Return on Investment (RoI)

This is also one of the most often used excuses, that there is not direct RoI through content marketing. The reality often times looks different and people who say this should rethink this statement. The power of content marketing lies in the clarity and easy language of the content that is created. These content pieces are created not for experts. This means that writing these articles means also scaling the reach of your potential clients and the people that you reach. More and more people are going to be reading these articles and get a basic understanding and support for your topic. Content marketing is like an accelerator that improves the possibilities to reach your next client. The more you create the bigger your chances of getting a return of goodwill from your readers, maybe there will be not a direct return on investment but in the long term it will definitely count for you and your business.

Obstacle #3: You're overwhelmed by technology

The good thing is that technology becomes easier and easier. In the old days, you needed coding experience and also skills that you have to train yourself within years to do this. Today software becomes as easy as your Facebook account and is very user-friendly. If you can handle your own Facebook or Instagram account then you can also learn to use software like Aweber, Kajabi, Mailchimp and other things that I will explain in this book.

Obstacle #4: You don't believe that it will work for you

If you're just starting out, maybe this is one of the toughest obstacles. You have to believe in yourself that you're going to figure things out. You have to trust in your ability that you will have some results at all and will get some returns. Some topics are maybe complicated for you and it all sound very tough but you have to believe in your ability to figure things out. Give yourself the time to learn new skills and acquire new strategies that will enable you to become a Content Millionaire again and again. These things are not casual and will increase the demand for your skills on the market, so don't underestimate the time that it takes to learn these skills.

Chapter 4: Content Analysis and Research

Let's start with the first step in order to create your effective content marketing plan. Analysis and research. This is the ground work for your success; if you do this work right, you will save time and money for the upcoming steps. You will achieve better results and also understand your target audience better. The more time you invest in the research and analysis part, the easier it will become for you in the further steps.

The good news is that it was never easier to collect data and find out about your target audience. In the old days, you had to outsource these kind of analysis to big agencies that created questions and interviewed people. Today you have access to much data that is totally free. Here are some examples how you can find quick and easy topics for the content to create:

- ○ **Amazon Reviews**

Amazon is just a great tool for gathering information about your customer. Type in the main keywords of your topic and read all the reviews about products like books or other physical products (the good and especially the bad reviews) and think in terms of how to fill the gap and create content that would serve these one star reviews. What are their needs and what do they need? The cool thing is that you can start a conversation with the people who wrote a review. Often times, authors who published their book on amazon get in conversation with one star reviewers and ask for feedback and ask more specific questions. You can do this too. If you've read all the reviews, you can start a conversation on the comment section with the people who reviewed the product.

Questions that you could ask one and two star reviewers:

- What do you expect from a good product about _____ (type in your topic)?
- What results do you expect as somebody who is interested in _____ (type in your topic)?
- What is your main goal for the next twelve months in the area of _____ (type in your topic)?

It is important that you check the products that are bought and often reviewed. Analyze them and ask yourself what makes them so special. Is there a way that you can deliver more value? Or do it in an easier or better way?

- o **Use Quora and national question forums for your research**

Quora is a question-and-answer website where questions are asked, answered, edited, and organized by a community of users. It is a powerful tool in order to find questions that people have about your topic of interest. After registration with your email address, you can search for your topic and find and cluster main questions. Use these questions for your copy in your content.

Quora is good for international topics but there are also national questions forums like in Germany Gutefrage.de. If you have a topic that is focused on your country you should primary research on this national question forum.

o **LinkedIn Forums**

LinkedIn is, in general, a great forum for content creators for several reasons. You can create for free your own account and use your profile also as a blog. You can create articles and share them on your profile. You can get in touch with like minded people very easily and network with people who share same interests and experience. In the section about leverage I will share you also a good way how to get in contact with A-players within your industry. In order to find out more about your target audience, start following LinkedIn forums based on your interest and start writing questions or commenting on blogs. It is again about finding more information about the needs, wishes and obstacles of your audience.

53

o **Facebook Groups**

Even when there is much criticism on Facebook about cambridge analytics and illegal data trading – Facebook is still a great tool to gather information about your target audience. Search for the five biggest Facebook groups that speak about your topic just through a basic research on the search place on your Facebook profile. The good thing is that getting in conversation with people is here much easier than on other tools. Important in all forums is one thing: Be familiar with the group rules and follow them through. Especially for big groups there are rules that are explained by the administrator. Often times an introduction of yourself is needed before you can start posting. After you introduced yourself let people know that you really care about the topic. Like, share and comment some of the posts on this group. People should be aware that you really read the posts and have a common goal just to make sure that you have a connection. They have to trust you and you should really care about their needs. Listen and read carefully, because their problems and comments are the copy for your next content piece, whitepaper and your next headline. If you focus diligently what they are writing about then you will earn their trust and you will understand what you have to create next as content piece.

- o **Google Trends**

Another more tactical idea to identify topics is a tool that is called Google Trends. If you have a gmail account, than you can do this for free. After creating your account you can sign up for Google Trends and make a reasonable keyword research.

This is especially interesting when you serve an international market because you can choose which market to look for. Want to serve the US market, then just click on the USA on the world view at Google Trends. The program automatically just focuses on results based on the USA. Want to get new clients in Canada? Then click on Canada and get the results there. The great thing at Google trends is that it shows you when your keyword is typed in at Google and when you also should focus on it. This sometimes is very basic. A periodical keyword is 'christmas' or 'christmas decoration'. This of course is an often used keyword in December but not that much in August. When you create a content plan you should put the keywords "christmas" and "christmas decoration" into December. This is just a simpified example. Often times, it is not yet clear which keyword is used, so your job is to find out which keywords are used the most and take it also into your content plan.

o **Google Analytics**

If you want to dig deeper with Google tools I recommend you to use Google Analytics. This is a more advanced tool that has a lot of power that you can use to find more about your target audience. You can find out if your visitors are using their mobile, desktop or tablet device, which social media channel are they coming from or using at all and at what times the users are most active. These information can be very helpful in order to optimize your content and deliver to your target audience. The thing with Google Analytics is that it can be very overwhelming if you have never worked with this tool. It is a powerful tool but you also have to take the time and learn the mechanics.

o **Content Analysis**

If Google Trends and also forums and groups are not enough one easy and quick way to find more information is a basic content analysis. A basic Google search can be already helpful. If you know which keywords are relevant for your target audience then search it on Google and look what happens. Read the first ten content pieces and also search for the news that are created based on this keyword. Read all these articles and content pieces that are build around your topic.

After you read all these articles ask yourself following questions:

o How are the articles structured?

o What is the headline?

o What are the sub-headlines?

o What kind of pictures are used?

o Which videos are included?

Answering all these questions will give you an basic understanding about which keywords and topics are relevant for your target audience. Just imagine you were in charge as Chief Content Creator and you have to create a new content strategy for your customer. Ask and answer following questions:

- What information that is not covered would you add to the content pieces?

- Which formats are used and which are not used yet that you could create? (formats mean: articles, videos, newsletter. In the section of content creation I will give you a deeper understanding about how to create it)

- What information would you delete from the previous articles because it is not recent anymore?
- How can you add a unique value that only you can add to it?
- How can you create an article that is combined with an event?
- What videos are included into the article and can you create better videos?
- Are their newsletter out there on the websites that you can subscribe to? How are the newsletters structured?
- Which experts are mentioned within these articles? Could you also get in touch with these experts and also quote them?

- What comments are people writing at the end of the article? What are their needs and what do they need?

Theses questions are not easy to answer but in order to create excellent content and make sure that people reach your content you have to be aware of them.

   o **Surveys**

Another very effective way in order to get a better understanding and gather data are surveys. I came over this the first time when I bought Jeff Walker's video online course Product Launch Formula. This is one main mechanism in order to understand your audience. There is a free tool called surveymonkey (just type in *surveymonkey.com*) where you can create quick and easy surveys and start collecting information. I'll give you an example how I figured out a product. When I began with video marketing I wanted to help authors because I'm an author myself and love to write (I think author's are the most important people that we have because they capture ideas and transfer these ideas to other people in written form). So I created my first survey at surveymonkey.com and created three basic questions:

- What is your biggest struggle as author?
- What is your biggest wish as author?
- What would help you the most as author?

I created this mini-survey and contacted authors on LinkedIn. It is possible on LinkedIn to filter the people that you want to see. I just wanted to see all authors and contacted them one by one. It was time consuming but it was worth doing it.

Based on these questions I got the three main struggles that authors have:

1. *How to publish and self-publish*

2. *How to market their book*

3. *How to sell their book*

This was great information for me because I knew exactly what content to create for my audience. I was not guessing and wondering around; I just knew their needs and what I had to do. One great thing about *surveymonkey.com* is also that you can capture email addresses which I would recommend you do. After answering my questions, there was an optional field where they can add their mail and their name. This was also very helpful in order to get in contact and ask deeper questions. I had around 60 authors that attended to my survey and more than 50 mail addresses. This sounds like small numbers but the truth is that everybody starts with small numbers. By the way: all big online marketers, content creators and also authors have some kind of email subscription where people can subscribe for.

- o Ask your potential target audience about their main struggle and wishes
- o Use *surveymonkey.com* to create free surveys
- o Identify the main struggles and also ask for the mail address of your target audience;
- o Use statistics and data

Even when you can create your own surveys and ask people about their opinion, you should check the official statistics. Sometimes they are free, sometimes you have to pay for them. The good thing is that there are so many institutes that are making researches and often times they offer help for free. When I researched about authors I found a survey and also asked authors myself about their main struggles. This can be also very powerful for your content creation strategy. Remember you can do a quick survey yourself and this means basically a connection with somebody, which is more important than just gathering data. Don't focus too much on statistics.

- **Wikipedia Research**

Maybe it sounds strange but you should also check Wikipedia for relevant content about your topic. On most searches at Google Wikipedia lands definitely on page one at Google and also often times also as first research answer. The reason is easy to explain: It is very good structured content and gives great overview about a topic. So, read the Wikipedia article about your topic and try to structure your article the same way. It's again about analyzing what is already created that works well and how can you implement these things in your own content plan? You don't have to invent everything new, you have to look first what is already on the market and then in the second step ask yourself how to add additional value or a unique and fresh perspective on your subject. This is your main task.

- Newsletter

Newsletter is a very effective way of marketing and can be also very helpful for your topic. What are the five most read newsletters within your industry? Are there any? You already checked the websites for your content analysis now dig deeper and look into more details about what are the newsletters publishing? How are they structured and which topics are mentioned? If there are no newsletters this is just a sign that there are not yet serious entrepreneurs who earn money with this kind of content.

- Youtube Channels

What Youtube Channels are the most seen and most commented about your topic? Sign up for them and watch these videos. What topics are they speaking about? What questions do they answer within their videos. How are these videos edited? Does it look professional or semi-professional? Can you do it in a better and easier way? Video marketing is a big thing and you should definitely think in one way or another about creating video content, because video is now more clicked and more often watched then ever before. If you really want to serve your audience you have to think about video formats either in front of the camera (talking into the camera) or as a screen-flow recording where people see your desktop (we will talk in more detail about content creation in the next chapter).

- **Podcasts**

What are the most famous and popular podcasts that people listen to? Often times the podcast host has also many follower and reaches many people.

What kind of questions do they answer? Podcasts are very popular because they are easy to consume especially in our smartphone generation. You can create much value with just little effort.

These were basic ideas how to structure your content analysis and your research about the already existing content. It is essential that you first make your research and dig deep into your topic before continuing with the next step. The more time you invest into researching and analyzing, the easier it will be for you in the next steps.

Main take-aways from this chapter:

- Before creating content invest your time intensively into researching and analyzing already existing content

- The more time you invest in content analysis, the easier will be the creation and you will be more successful in reaching your audience

Checklist for an effective Content Analysis and Research

o Google relevant articles and analyze their writing structure

o Search at Amazon for relevant products and read the reviews

o Use Quora for finding more information and basic questions

o Use Google Trends and Google Analytics for keywords and performing data about your topic o Participate at Facebook and Linkedin Groups about your topic and start answering questions

o Create a survey with *surveymonkey.com* and send it to people within your LinkedIn community

o Read and analyze the structure of the Wikipedia article about your topics and try to improve them with your own unique perspective

o Read some statistics that are relevant for your topic

o Sign up for your favourite newsletter within your industry

o Subscribe for relevant Youtube Channels and Podcasts within your industry

Chapter 5: Content Creation

After identifying the main topics and keywords of your target audience, you can start creating

your content plan. This is a plan that you ideally create once a year and follow through. The most important thing is to be consistent with your content plan and publish i.e. one original post once a week. After writing your content plan, there are many formats to deliver them to your audience. Basically there are three ways how to deliver content: in written form, in audio and as video. The specific formats of content are: Whitepapers, newsletter, videos, PDFs, ebooks, blogs and much more. Always focus on your target audience and what they prefer to consume. I will show you how to create and also name your content so that your readers will love, instantly identify with it and become raving fans of your content. We will also speak about how to create content in a very efficient way so that you leverage one piece for different channels and reuse them. We will also look at tools and software that will help you to become a content machine and use your time more efficiently.

However, first of all let's start with your content plan. This is a plan that you create ideally at the beginning of the year that makes sure that you go through all the content following a specific schedule. If it is not scheduled then it is just a dream that you want to accomplish, so you have to make sure that you have a written down plan. It depends on your personal resources and how much time you want to spend. So, weekly content is just not possible for some people, but monthly content is achievable for everybody. This should the minimum effort you make for the next twelve months. What are twelve topics that you're going to cover for your audience?

Based on the research from chapter four you should be very clear about the problems and struggles of your audience.

So write down **twelve main struggles or problems** of your target audience:

1. _____

2. _____

3._____

4._____

5. _____

6. _____

7. _____

8. _____

9. _____

10. _____

11. _____

12. _____

After you identified and wrote down the struggles you're almost done with your content plan. Now, your aim should always be that your content is going to solve the struggles of your audience. So, take the problem and formulate headlines that offer a specific number of solutions for the problems.

I give you an example to make it clear. One major problem of authors are low sales of their published book. So, this is the problem: low sales. Potential headlines for this problem could be:

o How to increase your book sales

o How to sell more books

o Five strategies to increase your book sales

o Strategies of Bestselling authors

I hope this point is clear. Now it's your turn. Write down **twelve headlines that solve the problems** of your target audience:

1. _____

2. _____

3._____

4._____

5. _____

6. _____

7. _____

8. _____

9. _____

10. _____

11. _____

12. _____

By the way it doesn't have to be twelve headlines. It could be also 52 headlines, for each week. The number of content depends on your time schedule like I wrote in the beginning. Twelve should be the minimum. After you've created the headlines we can move further to the real beef – the content itself.

In the introduction of this chapter I already mentioned different formats that are available on the market. Before going deeper into explaining all the different content pieces I want to give you a powerful tool in order to create content in any format. I call it the one-page content creation code.

The One-Page Content-Creation-Code

The audience that I want to help with my content is/are: _____

Which struggle of your target audience do you want to solve? (Should be ONE struggle/problem):

_____

The problem that I want to solve is:

_____

Write down three or four strategies/ tactics how to solve this problem:

Strategy

#1:_____

Strategy

#2:_____

Strategy

#3:_____

Strategy

#4:_____

I'm going to write this content piece on _____ (write down a date) and it is going to be live on _____ (write down a date). This is optional but you should write down a date because otherwise you will not take the time to sit down and create your content.

This is a structure that you can use for any content piece that you want to create. Define the problem based on your research and then give solutions for this problem. If you structure your content based on this format, then people will read, watch and listen to your content with more engagement.

Now let's start with the content itself.

Blog articles

Blog articles are very effective and a great tool sharing information with your target audience. You can create your article and publish it on a Content Management Systems (CMS) like Wordpress or on your LinkedIn profile (you can use your LinkedIn profile as a networking platform and also as a blog). We already spoke about your headline, now I'm going to explain more about content details.

When it comes to structuring your content, it is about being very clear about your main intention. I had one client who wanted to publish on Huffington Post and asked me if I could check his article. I did it and my answer to him was: "I don't get what you really want to say. It is just too complicated." Your main task when you create content is to make your topic easy and understandable. If you overwhelm people, they will not consume your content. So, don't try to sound intelligent, instead use easy words that are understandable for everyone. Make things easy and deliver also an easy solution with your content. If you have problems with creating content than follow my one-page content creation code where I break down the questions that you should answer for each content piece. You can use this one-page planer not only for blog posts, but also for whitepapers, for ebooks, for videos and also for your podcast. It is an easy and effective tool in order to create content and be very focused. It makes sense to use it for each content piece at the beginning; when you have more experience, you will do it automatically.

Before jumping into the next content piece, here is an example of how you can structure your blog post in more detail.

Structure for your content piece:

- **Headline: What problem to solve?**

We already spoke about headlines. It is important that you make clear that your content piece is solving a problem. Mention this in your headline. You should try to mention two things:

1. Who are you serving? and 2. What problem are you solving?

Good headlines:

How authors double their sales (1. Who= authors 2. What=sales)

3 Effective Marketing Strategies for Entrepreneurs (1. Who= Entrepreneurs 2. What=Marketing strategies)

- **Introduction**

After the headline there is a short introduction why this topic is relevant. Here you can mention surveys that are published recently, new case studies or a major shift in the market that changed the situation and lead to a new problem. After defining the problem, then you directly offer solutions for it.

- **3 strategies to solve problem X**

- Subheadline 1: First solution for problem x

- Offer the Solution

- Subheadline 2: Second solution for problem x

- Offer the Solution

- Subheadline 3: Third solution for problem x

- Offer the Solution

- **Conclusion**

Recap the problem and why it is relevant for your target audience. Shortly mention your solutions and obstacle that can come up during their journey. They should have these obstacles in mind when they start following your recommendations. This is the basic framework in order to structure your content. You can use this structure for your blog post but also for your ebook. The solution part within your ebook should be then longer, then in a blog post of course. However, the structure also works for whitepapers, your videos or your Facebook posts. This is one basic content formulation structure that you can implement in different formats when you're starting out.

Think about content more generally. What do people really care about? They care when you care about their struggles and help them to overcome them. This is something that your content should always have in common. Before writing or creating the content ask yourself: „Will this change somebody's life? Will this content take some pain or help somebody to be a more happy or lucky person?" If the answer is no then skip it, if the answer is yes then go for it and hit the publish button. Focus on the things that really matter and not some random topics that everybody else is publishing about.

Whitepapers

Whitepapers are PDFs that are created with a main reason like letting people know about a new survey. Whitepapers are shorter then ebooks, but longer then blog posts. There are no rules on how long it should be. Here again, you should be very specific about the main intention of your whitepaper, if this is going to solve the marketing problem of authors and increase their sales then name it like: How authors double their sales within two months. I have created my Whitepaper for authors. It was called Author-preneur: How to self-publish/publish, market and sell your own book. It is very clear which problems I want to solve with this Whitepaper. People love whitepapers because they are easy to consume on their smart phone, tablet or laptop. The good thing for you is that they are also easy to create.

Audio files

The great thing with audio is that it is not time intensive like written content. If you create a podcast then the only time you have to spend is in recording it. That's it basically. You don't have to change any grammar mistakes or something else, it is just the spoken words. You can offer podcasts or even reuse the sound of your videos as mp3. The good thing is that people can listen to it on their way to office or home. Audio files can also be the starting point for your content. If you organize an interview with an expert based on your field of interest then make sure to record it. You can transcribe this interview in written form and have already a PDF that you can use. You don't have to do the transcript yourself; you can just outsource it to a freelancer on fiverr.com (a platform for freelancer who work worldwide and share their services).

How to start and what format focus on?

This is a often asked questions: „There are so many formats, which one should I take first?" It always depends on your target audience, but honestly often times, especially if you're starting out you don't know what your target audience consumes. So, let me introduce you to this simple plan:

Short Tail	Social Media: Facebook, Twitter, Instagram, LinkedIn, Tiktok…
Medium Tail	Whitepapers, Blog Posts, Video Snippet,
Long Tail	Ebooks, webinars, interviews

Long tail formats take more time to create, this just makes sense. Try to arrange a 5-3-1 formula. For every long tail format that you create (you create one e-book), you create three medium tail formats (so one Whitepaper, one Blog post and one video snippet) and five short tail formats (two posts on Facebook, one at Twitter, one at

Instagram and one at LinkedIn). This is just a general recommendation in case you're unsure how much to create.

Another often asked question is which format first. It depends on your technical skills. If you have experience as video editor and also good equipment why not start with video blogs? If you already blog, then of course continue your blog and start to think in terms of what can add more value to your blog; maybe a newsletter that people can subscribe to.

Video:

Video is extremely effective because people love to watch videos. Think of your own behavior. Which would you favour? Watching a two minute video or reading a ten page whitepaper – the answer is obvious in my opinion (that doesn't mean that you shouldn't create the whitepaper by the way!). So, in general you have options on how to create your video:

1. *Direct into camera*

Means that you stand in front of a camera and deliver your content direct to your audience. Many people, me included in the past, don't feel good with this idea because they are too shy.

2. *Screenflow capture (where people just see your screen)*

You should do both and also mix them up. I had a lot of struggles with video because I wanted to make it perfect, which meant that I screw every video. It is very important to be in the moment when you shoot your video and therefore you have to practice.

Live Video

One effective tool is also live video: you can use Facebook Live or Youtube Live for delivering your message. People like real-time value and also love to interact with you and have the opportunity to ask direct questions in the chat. If you collect the questions, you can reuse them and tackle the main objections of your target audience. Make also sure when you create live videos to record them and reuse them as other products for example, for your video online course (as a bonus).

Video automatization

These days it becomes easy to create good video content and there are also many automation tools that work really well. Even your Iphone creates videos that are full automated. You even don't have to edit yourself! There are programs out there that will do the editing for you. Using these programs would mean that you first create shorter videos with your content pieces and then upload it on one of these programs. I will give a short overview which programs and tools you can use. Here are just a few:

Biteable: is great for all kind of videos. Doesn't matter if you want to create a Youtube video, a sales video or a Facebook advertising video. Use one of the frameworks that Biteable offers. They created video frameworks that fit with your special needs. What you have to do is upload your videos that you shot and integrate it within the tool. If you can use Facebook or LinkedIn you can also use all these tools that I mention here.

Animaker: is a fantastic tool if you're a fan of animation (like me). Especially interesting for explain videos for complicated topics. If you want to explain technical details these animations are just great.

Animoto: Create impressive videos in minutes with Animoto's drag-and-drop video maker. No video editing experience necessary.

Moovly: Create your explainer video, promo video, video tutorialor training videos with Moovly's online video editor and video templates.

Not all software is for free, in some tools you can create maximum of two videos and if you want to create more, you have to pay. Often times the free model is enough to create enough videos for one month. Pick one or two tools and try it! You will get immediate results. Important note: tools and software change! Maybe when you're reading this there will be much better tools out there which also are more interesting for you. The important thing is that you invest the time to learn the basics of these things instead of directly outsourcing video marketing to some agency. Please don't do this at the beginning. You have to get some experience with the tools in order to understand what is possible. After that you can still outsource it and delegate it to somebody else. If you outsource it before you really understand what you're doing how can you effectively manage the work-flow?

Often times your Iphone can create videos yourself even if you don't want it. Video automation is a big topic for Apple because they understood that their customer loves technology but are not interested in video editing details. This is just a great service they offer and cluster your pictures and videos based on your behaviour.

Webinars

Webinars are the opposite of live videos. Webinars are recorded videos that teach specific topics that are in a sales funnel. Webinars can also be very effective when it comes to teaching. There are also tools that you can use for. In most Webinars you see the screen and often times also the person who is teaching, but honestly it depends on the topic that you're teaching.

Video Online Courses

One great way to teach and reach people are video online courses. They are interactive, and people have a great tool for learning more about your topic. You can shoot the videos and then upload them on a Content Management System (CMS) and offer them for sales (More details about how to monetize your content is in the chapter about monetization). I personally love video online courses, you can learn whatever you want and the only thing you need is a laptop and internet connection. There are many programs out there, but you have to make sure that you nail the real needs of your target audience. What are their questions and what do they want to learn? Be very specific about what to teach so that you really shoot the videos that are relevant for your audience.

Udemy: Udemy is an online platform where you can buy and create every kind of video online course. From learning languages, coding to also more niche topics like investing in stock markets.

You can find any kind of topic there and you can become an instructor also yourself. My first video online course was at Udemy. It was really messy, but it was worth doing this experience and the same will be true for you. Sign up with your mail address and start creating your first curriculum at Udemy.

Kajabi: Kajabi is for more advanced people. If you really want to start a business with your own content, then you really need to sign up at Kajabi. Here you can collect email adresses, collect money, publish video online courses, your website and much more things. It is a great tool but if you didn't have already experience with other tools it will be too overwhelming.

Newsletter

Newsletter are great for getting in connection with your audience. It is fantastic because it is a connection between your reader and you. Some magic connection that people signed in by free will. When it comes to technical issues I recommend three different tools that you can use for starting with Newsletter:

Mailchimp: The free version is really a great tool for starting out. Here you can create optin-pages (these are pages where people can sign-in with their email address) and then deliver value to your email list.

Aweber: For several years I used Aweber and it is really a great tool for advanced marketers. Like in Mailchimp you can create great Optin-Pages and start collecting email addresses.

Kajabi: I already mentioned Kajabi in the context of video online courses; you can use Kajabi also for your personal newsletter. It is just a great tool for creating beautiful looking optin-pages.

Chapter 6: Content Monetization

So, I know what you're thinking: I'm creating all this content but how can I earn money with all this? You will learn about the money in this chapter. It is important to emphasize that first, we really focus on the needs and problems of your audience; if you do this the right way the money part will be much easier. Now let's start with the topic of how to monetize content that you generate.

Writing and publishing is easy for most people, but where it gets tough is the monetization,

because here, you need a basic understanding of business models. There are basically two business models how to earn money with your content:

1. You can offer your service as a writer or content marketer and generate content for a customer (which is time-consuming and highly competitive)

2. You can create yourself sales funnels and distribute your own content through

intelligent technology (you can leverage your time, money, and reach a bigger audiences).

Everybody is offering his or her service and changing time for money, but the second point is harder to achieve. You have to think about how to start organizing and offering your content in an intelligent way, so people can buy from you. Basically, what you can do is the campaign model: You offer free advice, and at some point, you can charge people for deeper training. That's basically how to charge your audience. When I started out, I made this without even knowing what I was doing. I was just so service-driven and wanted to offer the best results for my readers. I mentioned this already in the beginning of this book. During my Political Science study, I started creating abstracts that were two or three pages long. This was great for most students because instead of reading science articles that are 30 or 40 pages long they just have to read my abstract. Most students contacted me and said how much it helped them for their own study. Most of them were thankful for it and one person also wanted deeper training. She contacted me and asked me if I could give her teaching lessons about Political Science and I agreed. This is to some degree also offering a service, but it happened because I started creating and sharing valuable content.

Then I created my first ebook and all the time while I wrote my abstracts at the end I also included the link to my new ebook. So, every time students read my abstracts, at the end they could also get the the links to my ebooks about Political Science topics that I published. This is how it started for me. The good news is that through technology, it is much easier to organize your content in an intelligent way and also sell it. I will explain this further in this chapter.

The biggest mistakes that people make when it comes to monetization:

- **Mistake number 1#:** Many don't have an automatized campaign that leads into a sale: if you don't create a sales funnel and teach people how to do certain things, then nothing will change for them. This means you have to create a series of content pieces that help them to achieve their goal. If you want to teach somebody about how to create delicious food, then offer them three free recipes what they could cook. After these three content pieces make them an offer to your ebook or your video online course. Do you teach people how to create their own business? Then create content pieces about the quick start of starting an own business and offer your product at the end. If you don't have an automatized campaign, then you will always be depended on changing your time for money. If you do this, you will scale your business and your brand.

- **Mistake number 2#:** can't accept money on the website! This is a huge one! My wife loves to do jewellery herself, so I wanted to buy her something for Christmas. I bought a coupon about working for six hours at a local goldsmith. The thing was that I couldn't buy the coupon online, I have to make calls and write emails for the present and then send the money before getting the coupon. I thought, well in the 21st century normally this should be easier and thought about what she could do: accept Paypal on their website, book their schedules through an online calender that people could use. Minimizing the organization-related things would really mean focusing on her main job – creating jewellery. How about you? Can you create an offer and collect money from your website? If you can't it is really critical.

These days it is easier then ever, but often times it is really frustrating how many websites can't accept money. How can you earn revenue if you don't accept money online? You can at least accept money through Paypal which is in the most cases the easiest way to accept money from your audience.

- **Mistake number 3#:** don't have content products that fit with the target audience: This is also a no-brainer, but many people just don't have a product that they can sell. If you don't have any products, you can't sell anything and earn extra revenue. The only way to change this is to create your own product. Do you already have a product that you can sell? If not, your job is very clear. Go out and create your first product. It can be an ebook, a webinar or a video-online-course; it doesn't matter. The important thing is to start out and do it. If you don't make offers to sell your products, you will also not get any extra revenue for your products. It's that simple.

How to start your monetization:

After knowing the biggest mistakes about monetization, there is this question about how to start? Like I write before the most important thing is to create your own product but there are also other ways how you can earn revenue with your content.

- **Become a Thrive Global author**

Thrive Global, a platform that is found by Arianna Huffington, is an online platform where authors publish their own content. You can become an author there too and start writing about topics that are important to you. The cool thing is that you can also earn money there based on your topics and traffics that you get from the readers. This doesn't mean that you should do this the whole time, but starting to publish your content means becoming to some part an expert on this topic. If you want to establish yourself as Yoga expert, then start publishing about yoga at Thrive Global. After you've written ten unique pieces at Thrive Global and also gotten feedback by your audience, you can take these articles and create a whitepaper or an e-book on amazon KDP. By the way it doesn't have to be Thrive Global, it can be also any other publication where you offer your advice and knowledge.

- **Offer your expertise as public speaker**

One great tool for reaching a bigger audience is LinkedIn where you can start blogging about specific topics and use your profile also as a website. The good thing is that there are people out there who want deeper training and are also looking for experts like you. If you regularly blog about specific topics peoples will recognize you as an expert on this field and start asking questions. Collect these questions and answer them in a Q&A format and also offer the opportunity to book you as a public speaker.

- **Offer consulting service about your expertise**

This is one of my favorite ones because it is so easy to implement. If you have a Skype or zoom account, you can do consulting worldwide. This is the great thing about the web, you can easily reach a lot of people. Maybe there are people who want deeper training from you and need some consulting. You can arrange calls and speak with them about basic strategies and they pay you based on the time you invest. You can even do a group coaching where you have two or three clients and you speak about one topic and then have a Q&A. Offering your consulting is great because you're learning a lot about the needs and struggles of your audience and also get paid for doing it.

- Offer group coaching

Offering group coaching means basically that you have several people – at least two – who pay you for your expertise. This is a very lucrative form when it comes to coaching. You can coach a group of people through Skype or zoom and they also pay you. You give several lessons about your topic and also always organize a Q&A about your topic at the end. This will give you a deep understanding about your target audience, their struggles and problems. If possible always record these calls so that you can come back to them. This is also the foundation to creating your own digital product. The questions they ask are very important for your digital products, because they will give you an understanding what to focus on.

These are four ways how to earn money with your content. I know what you think these are all ways where I change my time for money, "I thought Yakup wanted to teach me how to monetize without spending more time to earn money." Yes, it is coming don't worry. If you do one or two of the mentioned things you learn a lot about your target audience and about their needs and problems. Now you exactly know what their big struggles are and you can create additional content that you can automate. You can create a video-online course, a webinar, a whitepaper or an ebook that you sell. If you speak with your client it is important that you take their struggles serious and also use their wording. One of my clients f.e. was not sure what is important for journalists, which topics to offer and which not to offer. So I planed a course about „*How to offer journalists topics that they love to take*". Based on the conversation that I had with my client I thought about a title that fit with their needs. You can do the same. It is not rocket-science, the important thing is to start. Even if you don't have clients yet you can offer your service for free at the beginning. I agreed to speaking gigs because

I knew it would mean new clients for me in the long-term, so I went there and gave an excellent speech and at the end also offered my help for people who want deeper training.

Once you know your target audience is struggling with a topic and you also know strategies how to improve their life you can start with the automation. This means creating content that people can consume easily. You can start creating video online courses, webinars, ebooks or continuity programs that you offer your target audience. Important is also that you start collecting email addresses in order to create a connection with your audience. Your email list is your baseline and the foundation of your marketing campaign. The bigger your list and the better your opening rates the easier it is for you to sell your products. Don't just send them your offer but also give value that actually help them to achieve their results faster and easier.

E-Mail Marketing

E-Mail Marketing is key for your own marketing plan. If you collect email addresses, reach out to your audience and have a good relationship your audience is going to start trusting you. E-Mail is really the key component in order to sell successfully your campaigns and sell also your own products. In order to have a warm list, a list of people that really like and trust you, you have to do the following five steps:

1. Subscribe for an E-Mail Marketing System (there are many out there on the market: Mailchimp, Aweber and Kajabi are only three systems. Mailchimp is for free, using

Aweber and Kajabi means also paying for them).

2. Create a PDF or a Whitepaper that solves a problem of your target audience. Offer this whitepaper in exchange for their name and e-mail adress.

3. Create an optin-page where people can sign with their names and e-mail addresses (if you sign up for one E-Mail Marketing System you can create one easily)

4. Start writing on a weekly basis to your readers and get them information that bring value (the topics to write about depend on your target audience)

5. Giving value and also offering your products for sale. This means that you have value emails (three or four in series)

and after your value emails you send them one offer. After your offer you start again with your value sequence.

These are basic steps in order to start with your E-Mail Marketing path. The bigger your list is and more people also open and read and react to your mail, the better for you. There are some things that you should have in mind when you start creating your newsletter content:

1. Personalize your content: Give details about yourself, your struggles and how you find a solution for it. People are interested in stories that touch their feeling. It should be of course true stories that you write about. People forget facts very fast, but good stories are things that keep them in mind.

2. Add a picture from you at the end of your newsletter so people see a face they can remember. Pictures say more then words. This is so true and especially in marketing terms as it is very powerful to focus on personal brands. In order to remember your brand, they should see your picture.

3. Think about the subject line. The subject line of your mail is the first thing that people see so you should be careful about it. It should be something catchy that get people's attention. Think of yourself as if you would get 20 newsletters on a daily basis. Which subject line would trigger you? Which would you choose for yourself?

When you warm up your list and send content on a regular basis than it is also time to offer one of your products. Things that you should remember here:

1. Set a clear deadline. How long is this offer available? If there is no deadline people will always think, well I can buy it also next week. If there is not a hard deadline there will be no sale at all. After this deadline is passed, something bad must happen. You have to take the offer away so that people can't buy your product any longer, or you must take some bonuses away.

2. Offer some bonuses. People love getting bonuses. Think about how to add additional value through one or two bonuses that you can offer additional to your main product. What are additional struggles that your target audience has?

3. Look for promotional partners. This means that you have to know who in your market is also collecting email addresses and selling products about your niche. If you did your research right at the beginning, then this will be very easy for you. Contact these people and try to work with them. I will explain in the leverage chapter how to maximize your success with promotional partners.

Start creating your first funnel:

A funnel is an automatized system that offers value and leads also into a sale. This sounds very complicated but basically it means that you give several pieces of content that helps your audience and then send them one offer for your product. Here an example:

I'm an author and wanted also help authors because I think everybody has a great story insight. So, I made a survey and asked authors about their main struggles. Basically, the three topics are: How to self-publish? How to market? How to sell? I created three different videos where I teach these three topics and after I send my readers to a sales video, where I also included a deadline. If you can automate this whole process, then you can make a sale while you sleep. In the moment when somebody is subscribing the whole process starts and is automated so that you can earn revenue without recognizing it.

Things that you have in mind when you create your funnels:

- You should test them before you automatize it. Just make sure that the content that you deliver really helps your audience. How do you know if your content changes people's lives? Easy. How many comments and thank you notes do you get by your target audience? If you really create content that changes people's life this will happen soon or later. This is also my personal goal for you and for anybody who is reading this book. That you deliver so much good will for your market place that people are naturally attracted to you.

What can happen at the beginning:

-   Your sales funnel may not work at first: This is normal when you're starting out.

You have to test what is working and what is not working. That's very important to remember.

- People will not buy. Don't take it personal. It is all about the messaging your product. Always ask other people if they really understand what you're trying to sell.

- People want to buy it later. This is also something that happens. People think that they can buy it later. Therefore, you really need a deadline where you take the offer away.

- People will not consume your product if you sell it. This also happens sometimes (specially in the marketing niche) that some people just buy products but don't go through it. It is like buying a book and not reading it. It happens, and you should not take it personally. Just focus on creating the best course with excellent content.

Becoming a Content Millionaire

I know what you think now: „The title of this book is Content Millionaire. When is he teaching that one?". Don't worry we're coming right now to this part. If you want to earn one million euro or dollar per year let's do some math first.

So 1,000,000 Euro (I just take Euro because my family and I live in Europe; but you can put your own currency into this formula) means 83,333 Euro per each month of the year (I just divided one million through twelve in the case this was to much algebra). 83,333 divided through four are 20,833 in each week. If you divide this amount through five, then you have the income per day that you need 4,166 Euro for each day. After dividing this amount trough eight you have to amount per hour for each day: 520 Euro.

So, here you have it again step-by-step:

1,000,000 : 12 = 83,333 is the income that you need for each month

83,333 : 4 = 20,833 for each week

20,833 : 5 = 4166 for each working day

4166 : 8 = 520 for each hour of the day

So, basically what this means is that you have to earn 4,166 Euro each day in order to become a millionaire. You have to create products that are worth this amount of money. If you think, I'm crazy and it is impossible to create so much value and products worth this amount than look to the top people within the internet business industry.

Products are sold for 2,000, 5,000 or even for 10,000 Dollar. Never underestimate what you can bring to the marketplace and what people are also ready to pay for. If you think the numbers are too big for yourself then divide them through two or through three but start somewhere. The biggest struggle is believing in your own skills and your ability to earn more money in the coming years.

So, let's start with an example how to earn the estimated 83,333 Euro each month. Here are some examples with different products that you can create.

You can create a Video Online Course worth 2,000 Euro. Create a Video-Online Course and launch it once a month. Let's imagine you have a list of 1,000 readers and it is also a warm list, which means people already know and trust you. You create an additional video online course and sell to 1% of your list. This means you have ten buyers out of your 1,000 email readers. You sold your course and earned 20,000 Euro with your video content. The next is your ebook. You created an ebook and published it at Amazon KDP without any costs. The ebook is worth 20 Euro and when you buy advertisement and sell around 1000 copies each month you earn about 20,000 Euro for this month (of course you will not keep 100% of this money because Amazon KDP is also earning with each sold copy, but it is all about net worth). Maybe you create also a webinar series that you sell for 50 Euro and sell 100 of them each month. The next thing could be group coaching, you can organize weekly or every two week online coaching sessions with one specific topic and Q&A. You can charge people for each coaching month 1000 Euro and with 20 people you already earn 20,000 Euro. The next option is a Master Class that you organize. A Master Class consists of fewer people that you charge higher prizes and that you coach more intensive. So, sometimes meetings are necessary for this kind of coaching, therefore there are only few seats possible. Let's say you accept four people into your master mind and charge 5,000 Euro for each person per month - that would be already 20,000 Euro.

Video Online Course: 10 x 2,000 Euro = 20,000 Euro

E-Book: 1000 x 20 Euro = 20,000 Euro

Webinars:	100 x 50 Euro =
	5,000 Euro
Group Coaching:	20 x 1000 Euro=
	20,000 Euro
Master Mind:	4 x 5000 Euro =
	20,000 Euro

Total monthly income:

85,000 Euro

This is just an illustration and it doesn't mean that you have to do all these things yourself. Maybe you even don't want to earn that much money, so don't worry. I just want to show what is possible and what you can do but it is not a must do for you. If your numbers are too high than divide them through two or four. What I important is to start!

Chapter 7: Content Optimization

Once you have published your content, you should think about it as an asset. An asset that is

growing in worth over time if you do the work that is necessary for it to happen. Think about your content like an investment that you make into the future. When you buy or build a house it is also an asset. You should think about your content the same way, because you already spend a lot of time creating it. This means that you have to do constant SEO (Search Engine Optimization). SEO basically means to structure your content that search engines, like Google, identify your content as a valuable piece. The good thing is, when you did your research at the beginning right, then your chances are good that SEO optimization becomes easy for you. There are basic rules when it comes to headlines, pictures, videos, and also Meta title that are included in your content, which is going to be explained in this chapter. Also, trends like Voice Search are covered in this chapter. The good news is that new SEO topics are always coming, but when you know the fundamentals of SEO, then you can cover every topic and reach your audience over and over again.

You should think about SEO optimization like doing Google a favor. Just think of yourself as if you would be Google or any other search engine on the market. How would you measure the value of a website based on the keywords that somebody is typing in? You would of course, as a search engine, choose the website that gives the most value. What are the parameters that you should check?

What is the headline?

What are the subheadlines? (These are the headlines within the article)

What kind of pictures are there and how are they named?

What kind of videos are there and how are they named?

How is the article structured?

Are there any downloadable documents that give the reader further information?

Is there social engagement?

Is the website user-friendly?

Is the website mobile friendly?

These are basic questions that you should ask yourself in order to optimize your article:

What is the headline?

The headline is key when it comes to online content. You have to make sure that your keyword is in the headline and is also a search term. How do you find out if the keyword has a big search volume? Just type it at Google and look how many people are also searching for this term. If there are only a few thousands it is not big enough, if there are around one million views than go for it. You have to make sure that your headline is found by search engines and this already starts with the headline. One easy way is to check which articles are read within the web and also check their headlines.

What are the subheadlines?

Subheadlines are important for structuring an article. It makes your point clearer and helps the reader to make sure that it is easy to consume. Make sure that you include several subheadlines (depends on how long your article is) and also use the keyword within the subheadlines. Ask yourself, if a busy reader who only read your subheadlines, would get the main message of your article? If no, you have to work on the subheadlines and name them differently.

What kind of pictures are there and how are they named?

Pictures help to understand a topic better and also helps to simplify complicated things. Always include pictures even if you just use quote cards for the articles. When I publish an interview I include strong quotes from the interview on quote cards. You can use *pablo.com*, which is a free tool, for creating quote cards and pictures for your article. The important thing is that you also name your pictures. It's very important that you include the main keyword into the picture otherwise Google will not recognize the picture as a value in your article. If you don't name it Google can't read it. You should not only include the keyword but also your name into the pictures to make sure than when people search for your topic that they also find you. The next time people search about your topic, you will also be identified as content creator and as the expert about this topic. This is important because search engines always look if content is presented in an easy and understandable way, so pictures help your readers to understand complicated topics easier.

What kind of videos are there and how are they named?

The same thing is true for your videos that you include into the article. Self-made videos are great and in the chapter about content creation I already introduced this idea of video automation and presented several options that you can use. It is always important to name your video also with the correct keywords. Otherwise the search engine will not recognize and find it. These days you can use different channels: Youtube, Facebook Live videos or even Instagram stories. In any case you always have to name the video with the correct keywords and don't forget also include your own name into it.

How is the article structured?

Your article structure is key. There is a reason why in many cases Wikipedia articles are mentioned on the first rank on the first page of Google – It is because of its easy and logical structure. It is structured very clear with a headline, subheadline, pictures and text. The easy and understandable structure of the wikipedia article shows Google that this is a valuable content piece. Always check the wikipedia page that is related to your topic and try to improve the already existing page.

Are there any downloadable documents that give the reader further information?

This is also an important question. You can add download links of documents within the article that give interested readers further information.

What you can do is you can upload a file in your dropbox account (also name your file like your headline or at least include one of the keywords in it) and offer the download link into your article.

Is there social engagement?

This is also one important factor. Google also ranks the social engagement for your content. This means you should definitely have a box at the end of your article where people can write their comments. Often times you can even add and write with your own Facebook account a comment.

Is the website user-friendly?

User-friendly means that people need less clicks as possible to get their main search results. The more complicated it is that harder will be to get their attention on your website. So, it is important that you check your website and try to do everything as easy as possible.

Is the website mobile friendly?

Do you check your website also in the mobile version? How does your site look like on smartphone? More user are searching with their smartphone online. since Google announced their "mobile first" strategy, it is a must these days that you create content that is mobile friendly.

Voice Search:

Voice search is a very young topic and is relevant because of devices like Alexa and Siri. Basically, what people can do is they can search for relevant information through their voice. Voice search is not yet a big thing, but in the future will be more relevant, so I just wanted to make sure that you already heard about it. Important when it comes to optimization of content for voice search is that you not only use keywords, but you also think in terms of whole sentences. Searchers are using whole sentences when they are searching information, so you have to make sure that the question they are asking is also your title. This is the first key difference. Another key thing is that you have to come directly with the answer to their question within the first paragraph. So, don't waste time and directly answer the question.

Meta title:

Meta title doesn't sound like a very big topic, but it is also key for your search results at google. You create meta titles on the backend of your CMS

(Wordpress or other CMS) and they are included on pictures that you use. It helps Google to identify if these pictures are really relevant or not for the topic that people are searching for. Through naming your meta titles in a correct way you make sure that search engines find you and your content.

SEO Tools/ Software

One big topic when it comes to SEO optimization is software for improving your content. These days content is data driven this means you need information about unique views, how many people click your articles and on which rank is your article or website listed at Google? The days where you once create content and never touch it again are gone. Today you always have to check the performance of your content because your competition does it for sure. Nowadays software tools mean that you have to spend money for it. Many people don't want to do this and say buying ads is easier and also more effective.

Software that you can use for analysis of your content performance:

These days, Professional SEO optimization means that you also optimize with software. There are many tools that you can use, which in the most cases means paid service. So, therefore I'm going to introduce some tools:

Searchmetrics

This tool is very powerful and gives also a lot of insights and information about your content performance. You can analyze your content performance and also create keyword cluster. When you create your content, this tool can also make suggestions which keywords to add and which to change in order to improve the SEO performance of your article. It is an ongoing process because once you published your article your SEO ranking on Google will change. Your competition of course also works on improving the SEO performance of their articles.

Google Analytics:

This is also a very powerful tool in order to analyze your content performance. Google can track basically everything that is relevant for you. Where the traffic is coming from, information about your target audience like age, gender, country and on which device they consume the content (mobile, desktop or tablet). The information is very valuable and shows also how many visitors you have each month, at what times most people consume your content. This information helps you to understand your target audience better and also create better content for them.

Optimization never ends

The bad news is that optimization never ends, and you always have to start from beginning because your competition is also optimizing. Once an article is ranked on Google at page one the race is starting, and all the other content creators are working to be on rank one themselves. They try to add more keywords, better content or try to get more engagement on social media in order to be higher ranked. This is a constant work for placing the first page on Google's ranking. Think of it as a competition with other companies out of your industry. If you stop optimization, then you automatically fall back.

Chapter 8: Traffic, Traffic, Traffic (Free and paid traffic)

After the content is written and published, we need traffic in order to generate buzz. In order to generate traffic, there are generally three ways: Free traffic (or also called organic traffic), paid traffic, and Joint Venture (JV) traffic. Free traffic is through organic search from your social media channels. When you post your content piece on your Facebook Newsfeed, your friends see this article. The reach of your content piece is at the same time limited because you only reach your friends on social media. In order to scale and reach a bigger audience, you have to buy advertisements on Facebook, LinkedIn, Google, or even start an Influencer marketing campaign. The third option is to create traffic through Joint

Venture partnerships. First, identify a Content Creator who serves the same target audience like you. Partner up with him, introduce yourself as a content creator for the same topic, and offer your own products. Now, let's dig deeper into how to do this exactly.

Prepare yourself for massive traffic

You must make sure that you prepare yourself for massive traffic. This means at the end of every interview, every blog post and guest blog you have to mention or publish a link that leads to a website which collects name and email address of your audience. Before you even create and do any of the things that I'm going to mention make sure that you first of all create an opt-in page that collects name and mail. Than start brainstorming and implementing strategies for increasing the traffic.

Free traffic

For spreading your content you can use all your social media accounts. It doesn't mean that you always reach more people, but friends will recognize it. Social Media is great for foreshadowing your own work and the projects that are coming. You should think of it like a big event that is coming and that you're excited about. The film industry is a great example. Before launching a new movie, there are multiple ways in order to foreshadowing the coming event. There are behind the scenes from the crew, there are interviews with the actors and there are also things that happened on the set that are worth telling. These little content pieces makes people excited and interested at the actual movie. Think of your products or content pieces the same like launching a big movie. You also have to think of smaller pieces of content that you can share with your audience. This can be accidents that happened and that changed the way you think, success stories from your students or obstacles that you have overcome in order to achieve your goal. It doesn't have to be big stories but it should be things that have meaning for you and that shows the audience something about your personality.

Social Media

Nowadays Social Media is very common. Facebook, Twitter, Instagram, Snapchatt, LinkedIn and also new trends like Tiktok – I'm sure you're very familiar with all of them. So, I'm not going to introduce them to you because I'm sure you know how to deal with them. The thing is that your personal social media channels generate you free traffic. The question is how to do it in the easiest way.

Buffer: Buffer is a great tool in order to schedule your social media posts. You can connect your social media channels with this software and pre-schedule your posts, and also choose when it is going to be published on which channel. There is a free version where you can schedule up to ten posts which means if you want one post each day you can plan the next ten days: https://buffer.com

Hootsuite: Hootsuite is another option for organizing and scheduling your posts. But this software has only a 30 day free version and you have to pay for this service: http://hootsuite.com

E-Mail Signature

Use your e-mail signature for your own marketing campaigns. Even if you didn't publish your book you can include a link to your site or your opt-in page and for-shadow your next book. If you already have the book cover include it also into your email signature. Try to use every channel that you have for your own marketing.

Paid Traffic

Paid traffic means basically that you pay money for one of the platforms, we're going to speak about, in order to be in front of your target audience. This means that you buy ads at platforms like Google, facebook or linkedin. Through paid traffic you reach people that you couldn't reach with your own contacts and free traffic. This means you can scale faster and also reach more people, and the good thing is that you only pay for your advertisement when people click your ad.

Google Advertisement

Google has the most experience with ads and therefor you can run very effective campaigns. It is also one of the more expensive ad campaigns that you run because of the CPC costs for keywords. If you want to run a global campaign, then Google ads are a must otherwise you're not really within the market.

Facebook Advertisement

Facebook ads are a big topic for itself and could be topic for an entire own book. Ads on Facebook can be very lucrative because you can reach people very targeted. If you know who you ideal client is than you can reach them very effectivally. You can choose which city, country, which sex and even how old your clients should be. This means many variables are possible to reach which makes everything also more complicated. If you exactly know your audience and keep also track about your ad campaigns and also track them well then Facebook ads are definitely the right place for you.

LinkedIn Advertisement

Linkedin ads are not as targeted as Facebook ads but they work really well for B2B. So, when you want to reach other businesses as clients than LinkedIn is definitely worth trying a shoot for your campaign. LinkedIn is worth using for your own content strategy because you can use your own profile as a blog and create a followership at LinkedIn.

Twitter Advertisement

Twitter ads are cheaper and you can reach a lot of people with your ads; that doesn't mean that your ads will convert for sure because they are not very specifically targeted ads like on Facebook or Google. But it is worth trying and giving a shoot.

Joint Venture Partnership

This is one of the coolest ways in order create traffic. You partner up with somebody who is creating content in the same field like you. This means that you work together and also promote each other's content. I know that you ask yourself why should this person promote my content? If you know how to influence other people you will succeed in this field.

First you have to understand what other content creators are trying to reach:

1. *They want to reach their target audience and help them*
2. *They want more topics and information about their target audience*
3. *They want interaction with their target audience*

This means if you can help with one or more of these goals you can work together. But what does this mean for you? If you serve the health sector and create content in this area and you want to win over this Joint Venture partner who is blogging about fitness and health, then you can offer a guest blog or an interview.

People support what they create

This is a term that I heard the first time by New York Times Bestselling author Brendon Burchard and it is so true. When you ask people for help and support and respect their opinion and create something together, than this is really powerful for both of you. One easy and fast way is through surveys that you create and ask for feedback. Before I published one of my e-books, I uploaded two versions of the e-book cover and let my community vote for the better option. People saw the cover, they recognize that you're going to publish something and so you create some buzz around it. You should of course respect the vote and choose the cover which got the majority – which I did. You can do this too or even start a survey at Facebook or create your own survey on *surveymonkey.com*. I would ask my social media community and also send my newsletter reader to a survey that I had created.

Guest blogging

Blogs are a great tool in order to reach your scale on the internet. It basically means that you create a content piece on a website which belongs to somebody else. Make your research and ask yourself who else is serving the same audience like me? Is there a way how I can follow him or her? How can I add additional value to the audience of this person? It is always about additional value – that's the key in order to be interesting for influencers. After identifying the key players within your industry try to add value in your unique way and offer your help.

Giving interviews

One great way in order to get your message out is giving interviews. I know what you think, who is going to interview me? Don't undervalue your own experience and your knowledge. In today world wide web, it becomes so easy to find the right people and share your knowledge because there are so many niches and through Skype or Zoom calls it is very easy to record an interview and then share it with an audience. If you made your research the right way at the beginning of the book than you know the experts and the people who create value. Try to contact these people and arrange an interview. You can even arrange an interview through *fiverr.com* where people offer an interview for their own show. This is something I made several times for entrepreneurs in the U.S. The only thing is that you have to keep the time difference in mind.

SEO Optimization

Make also sure that your online content is found by your readers through Search Engine Optimization (SEO). This means basically that you put the most important keywords into your article and also use them in your headline and sub-headlines. For effective SEO optimization there are two ways: On-page and off-page optimization – the first one means, you increase the SEO reach of your content on your website, the second one means to increase the awareness from other websites to your page. These days SEO means also additional tools like Google Analytics, Searchmetrics and also tracking functions otherwise you can't implement an effective content strategy.

Being on multiple channels

It is important that you follow through and use different channels for reaching to your audience. You don't have to be on every channel but you should focus on two or three channels that you constantly post value and help your target audience. It makes sense to be where your target audience is hanging around online. One great way in order to have posts in multiple channels is http://pablo.buffer.com/. On *pablo* you have access on thousands of pictures that you can use for free and directly use a framework in order to post them on Facebook, Twitter, or Pinterest. It is easy to use and completely for free. It's just a great way to get your content into different channels.

Promotion Partners

One effective way for increasing traffic are promotional partners that you include in your marketing plan and deliver value to your target audience. If you have the same target audience like the company or the NGO than there is this possibility to promote each other. You have to first deliver excellent content and show them that promoting your content would be a benefit for their audience. If they have a newsletter or a podcast series than you could suggest to be mentioned there or interviewed in their podcast. Through a promotional partner you will directly reach a bigger audience and will increase your brand.

Sweepstake

Sweepstake are just a great way to mobilize people for your own projects. People just love to win stuff. Even if you don't have a promotion partner in order to give away an i-phone you can give away your personal service. You can for example give away one-hour free consulting for three or four people which will generate buzz. Or create a Whitepaper related to a specific topic and give this away. One way to do this is to give away something for a comment on your blog or a like on your Facebook page. Always make sure that you get something in exchange which is useful also for you.

Affiliate Marketing

Affiliate Marketing is also a way how to increase your reach and it basically means that there are people out there who sell your products and get a deal. It depends on the deal but in the most cases it's a 50% deal. This means if you sell a product for 1000 Euro and Alex, who is working as affiliate marketer of your products, sells one of your products than Alex will get 500 Euro. There are different ways how to do it but in the most cases, your CMS helps you to arrange this. Your, so to say, recruiting workers for your products but pay them when they arrange a sale. They get an affiliate account from you and when there are promotions they will also be informed upfront.

Chapter 9: Content Leverage

As Content Creators, we are so obsessed to create new content that we didn't look at our already published content. In my opinion, already published content are assets that we have to check from time to time and reschedule in our daily agenda. If you don't have a strategy, this aspect will help you reorganize and rethink your already published content. Offer your expertise and your content to journalists, businesses, NGOs, and also podcasters in order to scale your reach. See yourself as resources for your topic and offer people your advice. Pitching journalists and becoming a contributor is also an effective way to reach a bigger audience and leverage your content. You not only position yourself within the media, but you also generate traffic from your contributor page from the media. As a contributor for Huffington Post, I can also add my social profiles and even my ebooks that I published at the end of each content piece that I publish.

Contacting the media

You first need this basic understanding that the media needs your content. Without you the newspapers would be empty, the radio shows would be silent and also the TV shows would be without guest. Journalists need Content Creators like us and our job is to write great press releases, which I will explain in detail, so that they recognize your projects. First things first, before even trying to pitch journalists that you know you have to be aware that you must first make your research:

Which publication is publishing about your topic? Which magazine, online platforms, blogs, podcasts, newspapers, radio shows, TV Shows are already publishing about your topic? This research is your first job and key for your success! You have to make your research and exactly know which publications are potentially interesting for you:

Make now your research and identify minimum five publications that are potentially interesting for you:

Publication #1:

_____

Publication #2:

_____

Publication #3:

_____

Publication   #4:

_____

Publication   #5:

_____

Everyone wants to be on Forbes or on the New York Times but the reality is that this is very hard to accomplish and you will not really achieve it before you have some experience on the ground. Which means start collecting experience on a local level. I guess in your community there are journalists from different news platforms that are hungry for your material. It is much easier to start on a local level because it is less competitive then with national or international news. I would recommend you start with the five publications that you have listed above and also start getting in contact with local journalists and offering your content.

How to get in contact with journalists?

First of all let's get a basic understanding what exactly journalists are doing. The main work of journalists consists of researching, meaning reading newspapers or magazines about their niche, interviewing people and also writing. That's it basically and they always have time pressure because the newspaper or the magazine has strict deadlines, which means when a journalist is working on two or even three big stories there is much time pressure to accomplish all three articles at the same time. They are at the same time constantly looking at new stories or ways to tell a story in a new way. New protagonists, a new context, changing environment or a new study are potentially interesting for them. So, this is important to remember because most pitches to journalists sound like this: "Hey, do you wanna write something about me/ my company/ my business/ my product", which is the wrong way to get in touch with journalists.

So, what do journalists want?

- They want to tell good stories
- They want to reach bigger audiences
- They are looking for conversation and also feedback about their content

So before you pitch journalists you have to warm up the relationship with them and get in contact with them. This means you must be on their radar and they have to recognize you in a positive way. There are two ways how to do this:

1. **Meet them in real person (which is most effective)**
2. **Meet them online**

Really, the most effective way to be on the radar of journalists is meeting them in person. If you start in your local community the chances are very good that you will meet them. Once a year there is a so called open day where people can visit the news desk and get in touch with journalists. Use this day and introduce yourself. Another option that I also used are workshops organized by journalists about journalism. Make sure to attend to these workshops and get in touch with journalists. This is in my opinion a must do, because journalists get mails and phone calls on a daily basis. They will always remind a conversation with a real person more then a simple email pitch.

The second option is to meet the journalists online, but there are also many mistakes that people make, that I will explain in a moment. The easiest way to do this is on LinkedIn in my own experience. This networking platform is super easy to handle and a great tool for reaching out to journalists. Here is how to do this: First you have to create your own LinkedIn account and start connecting with people. You can then send easily a connection request to the journalist. After that, regularly share the articles of the journalist, comment them in an intelligent way and also ask questions. Make sure that it is not about you, but it is more about their content! The more you really focus on their content the more they will come back to you. This is how I first be mentioned on Forbes Online as author. I first contacted and send the author a request and constantly liked and shared his content. Make it all about their content and then they will come back to you.

After you warmed the relationship and they already know and trust you it is time for pitching a topic. Make sure that your topic is something that is really relevant for them. It should be a topic which is NOT yet covered in their publication, a topic or a special niche that they haven't published yet. Again, this is very important, it should be a topic that is not yet published and I would also stress the importance of this niche and why you're an expert on this field. I'll give you an example:

When I pitched the German Version of Huffington Post I pitched with my e-book Immigrant Entrepreneurs and my basic argument was that they don't have articles yet about entrepreneurship and German policy combined with immigrant stories in Germany. Within hours I got my response by the editor and

I got my account as contributor for Huffington Post. If you make diligently your research then the pitch itself is the real easy part.

How to write effective press releases

Here are some basic rules when it comes to press releases:

- **Come straight to the point**

Journalists don't have much time. So don't produce poems and instead be clear and straight forward about the information. What is the main message of your press release? Why should the journalist take your press release? Is there a special event, anniversary, a new product or service? Within the first sentences the intention of the press release must be clear otherwise your e-mail will be deleted.

- **Shorter is better**

Often times people think when I add more information it is better, which is just not true! The more information you add the more work this means for the journalist because he has to read the whole article and pick up the relevant information. Be aware that journalists are working under time pressure and the more complicated your article looks the faster they will delete your e-mail. Of course, it always depends on your topic but the maximum is one page, which also includes contact details about you.

- **Send pictures and videos that are relevant**

Pictures are also important when it comes to newspapers and also online platforms. Make sure that the pictures have a good quality and at least

1-2 MB when you send them per e-mail. Videos are specially interesting for online platforms and can be shared through their social media community. The good thing is that you can upload the video on Youtube and share the link within your e-mail. Videos are great but make sure that you upload videos that are relevant for your topic and not send promotional videos.

- **Names are information**

This is one of the first rules that I learned during my first internship at the newspaper in my local hometown in Hof/ Sale: „Names are information". This means basically that you always have to double check names. Are they correct spelled? Is also the age added? Is the age correct?

- **Send it as early as possible**

This is a mistake that many people do when it comes to sending their press release. They send the press release just way too late. It always depends on the publication but earlier is better in my personal opinion. Magazines have the longest preparation time frame because they are so time intensive. For magazines, plan at least three months before the event or publication date – better would be starting reaching to journalists four months before. One month is enough for newspapers that are published on a daily basis. Online platforms that don't have a print version are also okay with one month before. Be aware of this fact and reverse engineer the publication of your article within the media.

I hope this already helps you for leveraging your content and reaching out to journalists. In the long-term this will help you a lot because journalists are multiplier within societies. One mentioning within the media can change your whole business because journalists read what other journalists are writing. Once mentioned within the media you will get more and more requests for being quoted or mentioned within other publications. Just imagine what would it mean for your business or organization if you were mentioned within the media on a regular basis.

Working together with NGO's and Corporations

This is something that can really bring you to the next level and scale your business. Working with

NGO's and/ or Corporations. The reason to do this is very simple:

1. **You can reach a bigger audience and get more traffic**
2. **You can get a corporate sponsor**

First of all it is very important to be aligned with the aims and goals of the NGO and the corporation. This means your content and you as person must be a good fit for this organization. This is true for the NGO and also for the corporation. This means when your main message is that entrepreneurship can change the world than a corporation that promotes and messages the opposite is not a good fit with you. To make sure that you fit with this corporation or NGO, you have to read the annual reports of this company.

NGO's also have reports that you can download and read them carefully. Try to understand what they are talking about and which aims are important for them? When you pitch them it is important that you use their language and also their terms. Show them how aligned you are with their goals and how this partnership would be a win-win situation for you and especially for them.

The same is also true when it comes to corporate sponsorship. You must convince corporations that you're a good fit for them through giving value to their potential customer. If you want to work with a law firm as corporate sponsor that focuses mainly on business cases, then n start creating content, which is related to topics for this target group. Content that gives them basic understanding about the topic and also solves problems. If you do this in a consistent way, you can become an influencer for this corporation and sponsorship would be the next step.

Influencing Influencer

The basic idea of influencing means just understanding the person in front of you based on their goals and wishes. If you know his/her goals and their passion than your almost done. Identify what they want to achieve and help them to achieve it. There are things that only you can do for other people. Think about how you can bring more value into the lives of these influencers. In my case it was always the media and creating content. I wrote articles and organized publications and mentioned business within the articles. This is for influencers, very interestingly, because they got quoted not only by me but also other journalists. Try to add value in your unique way and help other influencers in your own style.

Chapter 10: Main questions

This chapter is all about the main questions and struggle that people have when starting out. I don't know how much experience you have but some of these questions will apply also to you. Maybe all of them, maybe only some but it is better to be prepared. So here are some of the frequently asked questions:

Questions 1#: Why should I create content and share it?

Content is value for your readers. Content can be a blog post, a video, social media posts, MP3s or podcasts. The basic idea is to share valuable information through different channels. The great thing is that through the internet, you can leverage your content and reach more people instead of changing your time for money. Content Marketing helps us to get in touch with your audience and win new customers. Through content, you help your audience with daily problems and potential customer recognize you and your products. It's the first step to get them into your funnel and ultimately get to the sales.

Question 2#: How do I come up with content ideas?

There are many ways on how to get to your content ideas. Quora, Amazon or a simple Google research or https://answerthepublic.com/ will give you ideas. The most often read and commented articles at news portals like Forbes or Inc. also are an indicator for topics. Make your research and find out the top five websites about your topic. What are they writing about? Read as much as possible and ask yourself how to create additional value. How can you add value in your own personal way to your subject?

One very effective way is looking at mainstream news and using current topics and trends. If you f.e. write about stars and celebrity then you should definitely write about events like the Music Award or the Oscars. Using the mainstream topics doesn't mean just copying what everybody else is using but rather using the topic in a intelligent way for your own content plan.

Think about the ideal reader who is consuming your content. What are his or her main struggles and problems? What obstacles and challenges do they have? Try to solve these things and write a content piece for each problem and how to solve it.

Stephen King does this when he is writing his fiction books. In his non-fiction book "On Writing" he describes that he thinks often times as if his wife would read his book. You can also define somebody maybe also several persons that you write your content to. In marketing terms what you do is creating your avatar and writing specifically to this person.

Question 3#: How to create content when I don't have time?

This is also a topic that many departments have especially when they don't have much experience with PR and marketing. You should think about content as multiplier of your own business or your service. Through content you reach more people without traveling. You scale your business and your brand through your content. Isn't that great? I know, still many companies just don't have the resources. Either they don't have worker who create content or they don't have the time to do it. The good news is that it was never easier to create high-quality content. Here are some simple ways how to do it in a time-sensitive way:

- Organize an interview with an expert in your field and record this interview (you can do it with most smartphones). Take the audio file and send it to transcription to *fiverr.com* where they have actually people who transcribe your interview word by word. Voila and now you already have your first content piece.
- Outsource it to content creators or journalists at *fiverr.com*

- Define for yourself „writing time" and block this time no matter what happens. In my case f.e. I block the mornings always for writing schedules. I don't check emails or do other things. I'm focused and produce new content. In your case it doesn't have to be every day. For example, every Friday from 9-10 you produce new content. Be proactive with your time schedule.

Question 4#: How do I write so that people really consume my content?

Two basic ideas:

1. Solve problems with your content
2. Use SEO

Solving problems means that you solve concrete problems of your audience. What are their biggest obstacle and struggle? Research and survey about their biggest problem. Then create content pieces around these problems. Each problem is one content piece and gives several solutions for this problem. If you make sure that your audience really struggles with this topic and you create several solutions then it is just sure that your audience will consume it.

Learn basic things about Search Engine Optimization (SEO). This basically means that you understand how Google works. Use relevant keywords for your articles and integrate them into your headlines and sub-headlines. When you use pictures and videos then also name them and include the keywords so that Google knows this is relevant content. Basically, make your research and look at the top rated articles at Google about your topic. Which headlines do they use? Which sub-headlines and which questions do they answer? This gives you an overview how to SEO optimize your content.

Question 5#: How do I organize my content in an efficient way?

Two ways to organize your content in a more efficient way is mind map and also dropbox. Mind Map is very good for your brainstorming session about your content and your research. Just first make your research and write down all topics and headlines that you can find about your topic. This is your first draft for your content strategy and also your topics. Through this draft you first organize your topics. When it comes to the actual content use dropbox which is free and very useful. For each content piece create one file where you upload your text, pictures for your different social media channels and also videos. This is also good for resharing your content in a regular basis.

Question 6#: How often should I create unique content pieces? On a weekly or monthly base?

This really depends on your own schedule and how much time you have. The most important thing here is to implement some routines that you create your content on a regular basis. If weekly is to much pressure on you then start with monthly content. One long piece of content means twelve unique content pieces in the next twelve months. This is achievable no matter how busy you are currently. Define the twelve topics in advance and it will be easier to write them when the deadline is coming. When creating content on a monthly basis becomes easy for you then you can start trying weekly content.

Question 7#: What is SEO and do I really need it?

SEO stands for Search Engine Optimization and you definitely need to understand the basics of SEO. Basically you need to know how Google is searching and looking for value in the world wide web. Google is checking websites and articles and looking for the most valuable content and position them as search results. This means you should check the first page on Google based on your topic and research the articles there. Try to understand why these articles are so high ranked. What headlines do they use? Which subheadlines? And which pictures and videos are included? This research shows you what is working based on your topic.

Question 8#: I'm not very talented in writing should I still create content?

Absolutely, yes. Even if you think you don't have the writing skills of J.K. Rowling your capable of creating content that people love to consume. Maybe your writing skills are not that good but you love to speak. Than create a podcast or be an interview partner for a podcast. Record this interview and outsource it to somebody on *fiverr.com* and let them create your transcript. Whoala, you already created two unique content pieces – the podcast and the transcript of your podcast. It's easier than you think, don't over-complicate it.

Questions 9#: I'm not a techy person; can I still use all this software?

If you have a Facebook or Instagram account than you can also handle any other device or technology. It's not rocket science and the good thing is that it is getting easier and easier. Companies like Kajabi, Mailchimp and Aweber are of course interested in making things easier and easier because they know more non-tech people are interested in these kind of tools. They are constantly simplifying their software and upgrading beta-versions. This means that everybody can do this and nobody has any excuse not to.

Question 10#: How can I contact journalists and publish my content in the media?

The most important thing to know if you want to contact journalists is to know what they are looking for. Journalists are constantly looking for:

1. **New stories about their topic**
2. **Different angles of already existing stories**

If you understand what they want then it will be much easier to get in touch and pitch journalists. Let's take an example: If you are a business coach and want improve your PR then you should first know which publication you wanna be in. This is critical because most people just can't prioritize where they wanna be in. So, which publication do you want to be mentioned? After that you must read all the articles that are published about your topic. After you read all these articles you define what is missing and how you can add a new story. Always show the journalists that you're familiar with their medium and that you know who they targeting and writing for. You must give them the feeling that you exactly know what they are regularly publishing about and what topics they are writing about.

Question 11#: I don't feel good in front of a camera but still want to do video content. What should I do?

There are two ways how to create video content:

1. Speaking directly into camera
2. Creating a Screen-flow video

If you don't like to be in front of camera than you should try the second option and create screen-flow videos. These are videos where the screen of your laptop is recorded and people who watch your video just hear your voice. This is especially good for explaining things or showing a PowerPoint Presentation. The bad thing is that people don't feel connected to you because they can't see you. Speaking directly into camera creates a better connection to your audience because it feels like a real conversation.

Questions 12#: Why do I need advertising and spend money for online ads?

It is not a must do but if you really want to scale your business and reach more people than at one point you must decide at which platform you're going to spend money for advertising. Ads are nothing bad and you should think of them as Katapults for your own business. With them, you can reach people that you couldn't reach before, which is a great thing.

Questions 13#: I have no comments and shares of my content at Social Media. Why?

This is normal at the beginning and you shouldn't worry about it. Therefore it is important to reshare already published articles and make sure that you post them again. Over time your audience will grow and the people who came in later should also see your old posts. Don't worry that your raving fans will be disapointed because you shared already existing content. They are your raving fans, they love your content no matter what. You can also make small changes of the old content, for example change the headline or the pictures so that it looks new. Most importantly be consistent and start sharing on a regular basis content.

Chapter 11: Your first steps

This chapter is about your first steps that you can do. Don't overwhelm yourself from considering too much things.

Become member in Facebook groups where your audience is hanging around

I'm very sure that there is at least one Facebook group about your niche and topic. Use the search function on Facebook in order to find the group and send them a request. Read their group rules carefully and make sure that you understand them. Often times they don't want promotional content but starting a survey and adding value to their group is fine.

Start your first survey and ask people about their core problem

You can start your own survey at *surveymonkey.com* or you can create a survey at Facebook which is also super easy. The main aspect is that you ask for their biggest struggles that they have in their life and what would help them the most. Through these answers you're stepping into the shoes of your audience and your potential clients and understand their core needs. I often times also use their language that they are writing for my own copy. The chances that somebody else has the same struggle are very high. So, you're not only solving the problem of one person, but at least some dozen people's struggle.

Start collecting e-mail addresses

I already emphasized the importance of collecting email addresses. The moment you start collecting email addresses you really have a business, because the real power lies in the relationship with your list. What you need is an email provider like MailChimp, Aweber or Kajabi and an opt-in-page or also called squeeze page. This is a page that says basically: "If you want this FREE PDF/ Video series/ Podcast than subscribe here with your name and e-mail address". A squeeze page is a page where people can write down their name and also their email address in exchange for some value. This is basic step for newsletter marketing and helps you to get in touch with your audience.

Attend to seminars and surround yourself with like-minded people

One great way in order to lift your life is to change the people that your hanging around. One of my favourite quotes is from Jim Rohn „Your the average of the five people your hanging around with". So, be careful who you spend your time with. A great way to learn new people is to attend to workshops that are related to your topic. I love to go to seminars and workshops about marketing and network there with people. Direct interaction is often times more valuable than consuming a video online course.

Look for JV partners and add value to them

Your not the first person who is working in your niche. There are also other entrepreneurs who are also passionate about your subject and may be teaching it in a different way. Start identifying them and getting in contact with them. In the long term these people are good fits for your future promotions. So, help them share their posts, increase their number of email subscribers or help them with relevant information. Don't see them only as business rivals, rather think about how to bring additional value to the market place and give information that is compatible.

Start creating videos every week

People love to consume videos and click them. So make sure that you also regularly create some videos that add value to your audience. It doesn't have to be long videos but it should focus on solving problems and how-to-advice for your audience. You can create videos and speak directly into the camera or you create screen-flow videos where people see the screen of your laptop and hear your voice. The second video style is especially good if you explain things and also show how things work out. If you have a Mac than it is very easy to create video with QuickTimePlayer. You can create both versions with your mac. You can record yourself with the camera within the computer and also record your screen and upload it as video.

Use different social media channels

Your audience is very heterogeneous and they like to consume your content within different channels. That's okay and you have to have this in mind when you create your content. You don't have to be on every social media channel but just make sure that you focus at two channels at least.

If you have a Facebook account and regularly post their then also start additionally your Videoblog at Youtube.

Start creating digital products that you can sell

Basically, this means that you have to have an offer. Think about digital products like creating your first asset that is printing money for you. Otherwise you will always change your time for money. So, start focusing on assets that people really need. There are many ways how to create digital products. You can create ebooks, webinars, video online courses or membership sites. It always depends on what is easier for you to create and what your audience is interested in.

Chapter 12: Final chapter

Congratulations, we`re almost done. You learned a lot of things during the last chapters. The important thing is to implement the strategies in order to become a content millionaire. Like I wrote in the beginning of this book; it is all about how to change the life of your target audience in a positive way and also generate a fortune on the way. If you deeply care about your audience and focus on their struggles with your content, they will love to consume your content.

I just want to say thank you for reading this book. For me it is a honor that you spent your valuable time reading it and I really appreciate this. Always remember that it is not about you or me, it is always about our audience, about their struggles and dreams. If you communicate this in your content they will love to consume your content. Hope this serves and helps you.

Best wishes

Ceyhun Yakup Özkardes-Cheung

www.ingramcontent.com/pod-product-compliance
Lightning Source LLC
Chambersburg PA
CBHW030623220526
45463CB00004B/1396